THE CROMFORD & HIGH PEAK RAILWAY IN COLOUR

John Evans

AMBERLEY

Dedication

Over the years many people have said I should publish my colour photographs of the Cromford & High Peak line and I am very grateful to the team at Amberley Publishing for making this possible.

This book is in memory of one of the three boys mentioned in the introduction – Alistair Kohler, who sadly passed away three years ago.

First published 2017

Amberley Publishing
The Hill, Stroud
Gloucestershire, GL5 4EP

www.amberley-books.com

Copyright © John Evans, 2017

The right of John Evans to be identified as the Author of this work has been asserted in accordance with the Copyrights, Designs and Patents Act 1988.

ISBN 978 1 4456 6408 8 (print)
ISBN 978 1 4456 6409 5 (ebook)

All rights reserved. No part of this book may be reprinted or reproduced or utilised in any form or by any electronic, mechanical or other means, now known or hereafter invented, including photocopying and recording, or in any information storage or retrieval system, without the permission in writing from the Publishers.

British Library Cataloguing in Publication Data.
A catalogue record for this book is available from the British Library.

Typeset in 10pt on 13pt Celeste.
Typesetting by Amberley Publishing.
Printed in the UK.

Foreword

To some readers 1967 will seem a far off era. It was indeed half a century ago, but exciting things were taking place; men were within a couple of years of landing on the moon, colour television broadcasts started, and Hewlett Packard had recently launched their first computer. But while technology was moving on apace there was, tucked away in the Derbyshire hills, a railway carrying on its unique operation much as it had done for the last 136 years. This was the year that the Cromford & High Peak Railway finally closed, but not before it had captivated the imagination of many, including the author, John Evans, and he in turn had introduced it to myself.

These were exciting – not to mention challenging – times for anyone with an interest in the industrial heritage of our country and particularly its railway systems. Things were changing fast and there was so much to see before it vanished forever, or so we feared. Things reached frenzy pitch for us in the middle of the sixties when railways all over the country were closing in the wake of Beeching and steam power of all sorts was disappearing rapidly. Where to go next? Should we find the last push pull train in the area? Travel on the *Bournemouth Belle*, one of the last steam-hauled express trains? Pay our last respects to the Somerset & Dorset line? My photographic diary for April 1967 records that in one week John and I visited Bedford to photograph St John's station, Silverstone motor racing circuit (how did that get in there?), some locations on the partially closed Northampton to Wellingborough line, a couple of ironstone quarries still running steam locos, the Cromford & High Peak (of course!), and a day working on the derelict waterworks beam engine that we had adopted. Luckily John was able to run a Fiat 600 and we both had – within the budget constraints of the time – reasonable cameras.

The Cromford & High Peak has always been special to John. Was it the steam locos, the inclines and their unusual working practices, or that intriguing signal perched high up on the hill that could be seen for miles around? It even had a beam engine! Personally, I shall be forever in his debt for re-introducing me to the line after a gap of almost fifty years. But things are different now; then it was all about the engines and the ancient railway equipment – now I see it in the context of the amazing Derbyshire landscape. I admire – in a way I didn't all those years ago – the stupendous accomplishment of the men who built the line through this challenging terrain. This is an old railway; very old – the first section was opened in 1830. That's the same year as the Liverpool & Manchester Railway opened and seven years before Victoria came to the throne! Take yourself to

Minninglow on the High Peak Trail, walk to the far end of the great stone embankment and look back. This is no graceful Ribblehead Viaduct crossing the landscape, but a mighty bulwark in the finest medieval tradition.

John's love for this railway shines through in this book. If you knew it in its working days memories will be rekindled. If you have walked or cycled the High Peak Trail or the Midshires Way, it will give you an insight into what was there before. Above all it will introduce you to this most unusual railway that once ran through an outstandingly beautiful part of our wonderful country.

I hope you enjoy it as I have.

Bryan Jeyes
Great Coates, North East Lincolnshire, October 2016

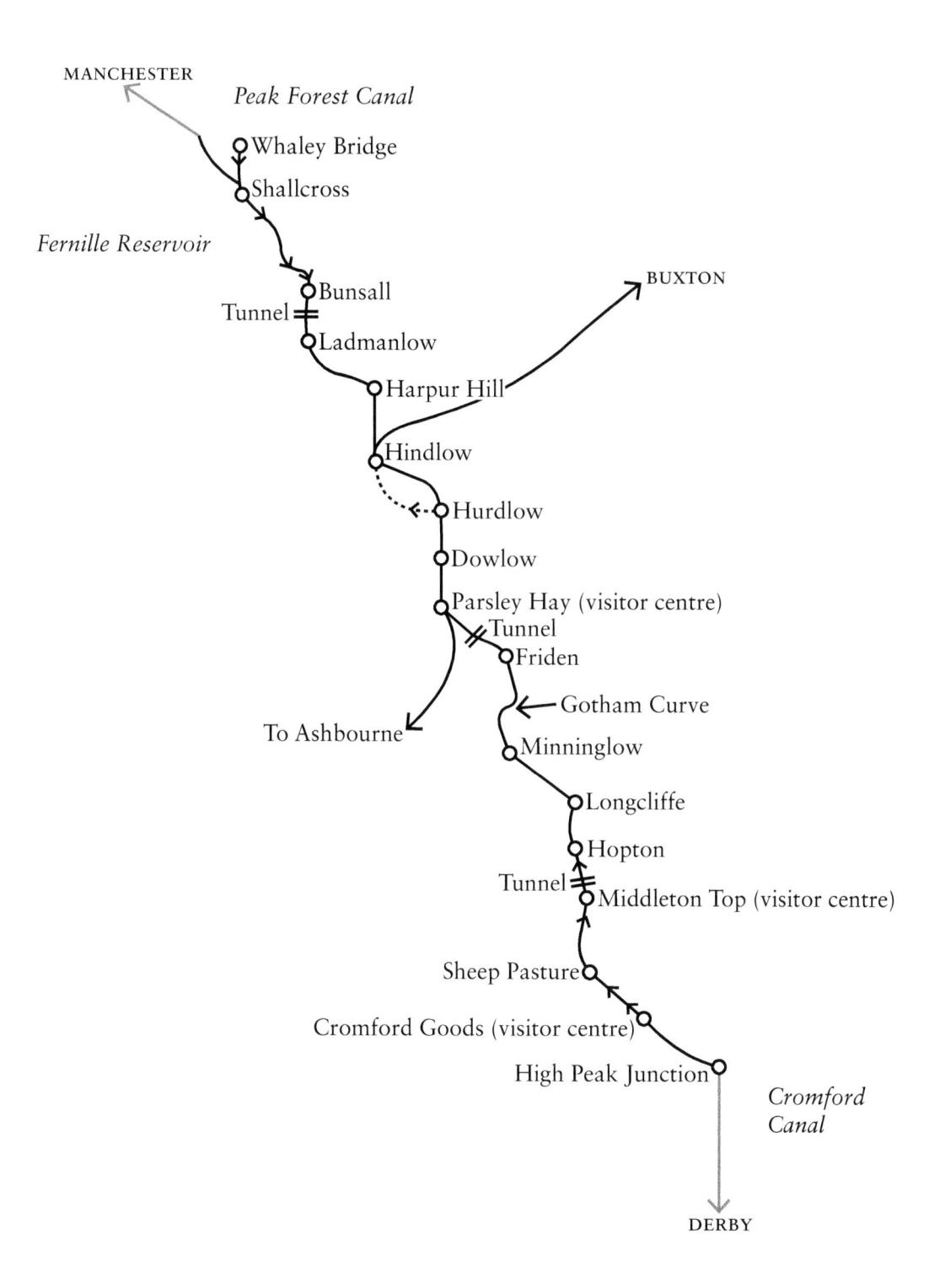

MANCHESTER

Peak Forest Canal

Whaley Bridge
Shallcross

Fernille Reservoir

Tunnel
Bunsall
Ladmanlow
Harpur Hill

BUXTON

Hindlow
Hurdlow
Dowlow
Parsley Hay (visitor centre)
Tunnel
Friden
Gotham Curve

To Ashbourne

Minninglow
Longcliffe
Hopton
Tunnel
Middleton Top (visitor centre)
Sheep Pasture
Cromford Goods (visitor centre)
High Peak Junction

Cromford Canal

DERBY

5

Introduction

On a dull but warm August afternoon in the early 1960s, three schoolboys stand on Derby station, chatting about the trains that are passing. They wear the classic trainspotters' uniform of shirts and ties with grey flannels and carry a duffel bag containing the remnants of their lunch, plus a copy of the latest *Ian Allan ABC* listing all the engines in service on British Railways. All three are in possession of what is called a 'runabout' ticket costing seven shillings and sixpence (37.5p) – a seven-day pass to use a network of trains all over the East Midlands. They have worked out a hectic timetable that enables them to cover every line in the area in one week and today they are hoping to touch the northern tip – the station at Matlock, in the Derbyshire Peak District.

'Derby, Derby, this is Derby.' The familiar flat voice of the station announcer is then mimicked by the boys, who burst into laughter. Although quite a few passenger trains are now diesel-hauled, nearly all the freights are powered by steam engines, and an endless procession of them passes along the through lines in front of the locomotive works.

At last a train to Manchester approaches. It's this service that the boys will catch as far as Matlock – new territory for all of them. A dark green 'Peak' diesel runs into the station throbbing noisily and the boys jot down its number before it stops. They clamber into the third coach, which has individual compartments, hoping they won't be joined by any other passengers. Their luck is out, however, and a tall lad with an open-neck shirt, unruly hair, and a breezy air about him joins the trio. Soon they get talking. All four share something in common – a fascination for railways. So they swap stories as the guard's whistle blows, allowing the Peak diesel to rev its engine and glide smoothly northwards from Derby station. The conversation pauses as all four boys write down the number of a wheezy old Fowler 0-6-0 moving south with a short freight, and the train rattles over crossings and points before accelerating towards the undulating countryside.

It's obvious to the three boys that the newcomer knows the Derby to Manchester main line well. He explains that he lives in Manchester and that a ride to Derby on the old Midland Railway main line is one of his favourites. It boasts lovely scenery, a host of tunnels and viaducts, and lots of gradients to test the energy levels of both crew and locomotive.

'Of course,' he explains, 'it's not the same with diesels. They need no coaxing up the hills. It always used to be a "Jubilee" on this run. Still is sometimes.' Steam's old magic continues unabated.

The train rumbles northwards and the visitor points out lineside features, locations with potential for seeing trains, and places of interest. The first of these is Ambergate station.

'It's a triangle,' he explains. 'Very unusual. We are approaching from the south and will continue northwest to Matlock and Manchester, but we could divert northeast to Chesterfield and Sheffield. Where the lines meet they form a triangle and Ambergate has six platforms serving each side of the triangle. Look out for a freight coming from the Sheffield direction and following us towards Matlock.'

Sure enough, as they glance out of the window they see a Stanier 8F with a load of hopper wagons at the north end of the station waiting for the diesel to pass so it can follow behind.

'You should get off at Ambergate some time,' says the Mancunian. 'Worth it, honest. You'll be seeing trains all day.'

As soon as Ambergate is passed, the countryside becomes much more dramatic. The four tracks become two and are enclosed with dense trees, cuttings and rocky outcrops. A small station delights in the unusual name of Whatstandwell as the train rushes northwards.

'High Peak Junction coming up next on your left,' announces the boy importantly. Eager eyes peer at a few sidings with loaded wagons, but no locomotives are seen.

'You can sometimes spot a tank engine there,' says the boy. 'Next thing is the signal on the hill. Up there, can you see it?' I stare upwards (you probably guessed that one of the threesome was me) but can see nothing resembling a signal. Why would there be a signal on a hill top anyway? The train then races over a bridge, enters a station, and immediately plunges into a tunnel.

'Did you see it – that signal?' I ask Bob.

'I think so,' he replies unconvincingly, but Alistair is sure he's seen it.

'We can look again on our way back,' suggests Alistair. Meanwhile the train is beginning to slow down.

'What is a signal doing on top of a hill?' Alistair asks.

'It's the Cromford & High Peak line,' he replies. 'It's an amazing secret railway that crosses the top of the hills. It's the best railway you could ever find and yet no-one knows about it. Get off the train at Cromford station and you'll find it. They even have winding engines to haul wagons up the hills with ropes, they are that steep. Go and see it.'

The train grinds to a halt and the three boys gather together their belongings, say farewell, and offer thanks to their new friend. Then they jump out on to Matlock's platforms, waiting for the next train to take them back to Derby. This was to be a very short visit.

On the way back, they are on a stopping train, which conveniently halts at Cromford station. No dismounting today for the lads, but the coach is buzzing with excitement. What kind of railway can it be that pulls wagons up hills on ropes? They'd seen pictures of this sort of thing, but surely they all closed down years ago?

'Never mind pulling wagons on ropes, was he pulling our legs?' I ask.

But the answer comes as we move gently away from Cromford station. There, clear for us all to see, is a tiny signal, perched high up on the side of a hill. Plans are immediately changed. Saturday, the last day of our runabout week, will no longer be spent shuttling between Nottingham Victoria and Nottingham Midland. We will go back to Cromford and try to find a different kind of railway adventure.

Bryan, Alistair and the author (with my camera set on its self-timer) at Middleton Top on 30 June 1966. We are all correctly wearing ties for a day photographing trains and Bryan has the essential Weston Master invercone attached to his camera strap.

Brief Encounter

True to our revised plans we found ourselves standing on the platform at Cromford two days later. Apart from the fact that the station had a tunnel mouth at its northern end, the buildings were impressive – apparently the work of some fanciful architect. They seemed as though they had been plucked from the grounds of a French chateau. We walked out of the station, having asked the way to the High Peak line. A vague arm pointing south was the only direction we received and we walked along paths and got hopelessly lost. Returning to the station, we then strode along the main A6 road in a southerly direction for about a mile and, as we approached a short row of houses, a bridge appeared. Sure enough, a very steep railway line ran beneath it. We eventually found our way to what we came to know as Cromford Bottom, where we found a cluster of wagons, old sheds, a wharf next to an overgrown canal and, tucked away in its shed, a tiny 0-4-0 saddle tank – No. 47007. Climbing upwards at a crazy gradient were two tracks that passed beneath the main A6 road. In the centre of each track was a sturdy wire rope. There was no-one about. A few wagons streaked in some kind of white solution waited in sidings, alongside a couple of antique locomotive tenders.

'It's a Saturday,' said Bob. 'Maybe they don't work on Saturdays.'

To find that signal on the hill we needed to go uphill. We decided to climb the fierce gradient, watching out in case the wire rope suddenly moved. Much of the line was enclosed in a tight cutting. It was fascinating to think of trains actually moving on rails this steep and we had a good laugh at a gradient post saying '1 in 8', but we saw nothing move. After a great deal of energy had been expended, we found ourselves at the top, where the lines levelled out and ran straight past a cluster of buildings. Here, No. 47006 – a sister to No. 47007 – was in very light steam, and near the engine was a signal – the one we had seen the previous day from our train far below. Walking further on for about half an hour, we eventually reached another incline, mercifully shorter, and at the top found a winding engine and a grubby J94 0-6-0 saddle tank – No. 68079, also in light steam.

The return walk took a couple of hours, but such was our fascination with the introduction to this anachronistic railway, we all decided this was the start of an adventure, not the conclusion. Sometimes together, later with another friend, Bryan Jeyes, we made regular visits to the Cromford & High Peak Railway. Once in possession of a car, we explored the whole line from Cromford to Whaley Bridge on more than one occasion, including sections long since closed, clutching our precious cameras and that costly transparency film.

This volume is unusual in that it shows the line in colour. Not only did the High Peak Railway have relatively few visitors – especially considering it was a unique survivor – but it led a kind of hidden existence, getting on with its business in a wonderfully primitive nineteenth century way while the rest of the railway network went through the tumult of 1960s modernisation. I imagine that one day someone at Euston noticed this funny line on a map and wondered what was going on in that remote part of Derbyshire. Once he found out he sadly decided it was too expensive to run, had little and declining business, and should be expunged from Britain's new railway. Yet, if he thought that was the end, he grossly underestimated the High Peak line's survival instinct. Today as the High Peak Trail it attracts people in numbers impossible to conceive in its working days, providing a wonderful amenity for cyclists and walkers. The tracks may have gone, but the spirit most certainly remains.

Why was it Built?

Two canals were the catalyst that gave birth to the Cromford & High Peak Railway. There has always been an inseparable link between canals and railways. Sometimes, they twist and turn in a knotty tangle along a valley, often joined by a road or a river as well. The canal companies pioneered many of the routes which the railways later used to steal the canal-carriers' trade. It is certainly the case with the Cromford Canal, which shares a tight valley with the main A6 road, the River Derwent, and what was once the Midland Railway's main line from Derby to Manchester – now a humble single track branch line to Matlock.

The Cromford Canal was built to haul coal, but also served local quarries, lead works, agriculture and mills. In the general enthusiasm for railways, which had their mania for construction during the mid-nineteenth century, we sometimes forget that in the late eighteenth century there was a similar passion to build canals. Speculators were eager to invest in a network of waterways that linked the whole of Britain. Although canal travel seems (and is) very slow, it has to be compared with the other method of transport available in those days: the horse and cart. Not only was this even slower, but a cart held a fraction of the load possible with a canal boat, so canal travel was cheap and relatively efficient.

The Cromford Canal was a fourteen-mile extension north from the Erewash Canal in Nottinghamshire, which connected with the rest of the Midlands canal network. The builders had to overcome several engineering problems but, once opened in 1794, it was very successful shifting coal, textiles and limestone in the Derwent Valley southwards. Eventually it was purchased by a railway company, which had built a line adjacent to the canal and started to take away its trade. From the middle of the nineteenth century, traffic started to decline. Its main engineering feature was the 2,600-metre-long Butterley Tunnel, which at the time was one of the longest in the world, but the tunnel suffered continual problems – eventually being permanently closed after a collapse at the turn of the century. From that point, the canal was split into two with the northern section from Ambergate to Cromford being isolated – a distance of around five miles. Even so, it continued in use for many more years, handling mainly local coal traffic. It was eventually abandoned by British Waterways in 1944, but part of it near Cromford has been restored by enthusiasts. They hope to re-open the whole length – much of which has disappeared – including re-opening Butterley tunnel: a frightening challenge.

The Peak Forest Canal

What of the northern end? The waterway there was the Peak Forest Canal, which ran from Whaley Bridge to Manchester and was a noted limestone carrier. Its construction had been fraught with engineering difficulties, but it finally opened in 1800. If you look at an old gazetteer of Britain's canal system, you can see two dead-ends in north Derbyshire. Pointing south was the Peak Forest Canal, which terminated at Whaley Bridge; pointing north was the Cromford Canal. The idea of linking the two looks as obvious today as it did back in the early nineteenth century.

A distance of around thirty miles separated the two canals, but it was the terrain rather than the distance which was the main obstacle to those seeking to connect those two 'dead ends.' The initial thoughts centred naturally on constructing another canal, but the porous limestone over which it was to be built wouldn't hold water. There were also engineering challenges with the canal scheme, especially in maintaining a supply of water – the lifeblood of a canal. The landscape was hilly, rugged and wild and would require an army of locks.

Here's one of my favourite diesel pictures. It shows Sulzer Type 2 No. D5228 in immaculate condition heading north along the main line towards Cromford on 13 April 1967. Leawood Pump House is in the centre of the picture; Lea Wood Tunnel is in the background and Cromford Wharf is to the right. The train comprises an inspection saloon.

A Unique Railway

The alternative proposal was for a railway like no other built in this country. The line was to be built on canal principles, with level sections interconnected by a series of steep gradients surmounted not with locks, but by rope-worked inclines. Between the inclines, horses pulled the wagons. The inclines employed steam winding engines that would haul wagons up the gradients attached to ropes. These inclines raised the line by around 300 metres (1,000 feet) to its summit near Ladmanlow, followed by more inclines providing a steep descent to Whaley Bridge. The total length was thirty-three miles and by July 1831 it was open. The time to transport freight from Cromford to Whaley Bridge was two days. Discover the area and you will realise how much longer it must have taken by the alternative – horses and wagons.

Just consider for a moment the engineering achievement in building this railway. We are really at the dawn of railway construction – the first long distance trunk line was still seven years away. Starting at Cromford, much of the hard climbing work was completed in the first five miles, where the line initially rose by two inclines from Cromford to Sheep Pasture and then proceeded on the level to the bottom of another incline at Middleton. After this, the rails were then fairly level again before passing through a tunnel and facing a further incline at Hopton. This meant four steam-worked inclines in just a few miles, with another incline at Hurdlow, halfway along the line. After a level stretch, they were followed by four more (downhill) inclines to return trains to canal level at Whaley Bridge. The Whaley Bridge incline differed from the others because it was operated by a horse-drawn gin, or windlass, on a system that had been used in coal mines to haul loads up from the pit. Here the wagons were unloaded and the loads resumed their journey to the north on canal boats.

On the level sections worked by horses, it wasn't long before animal power gave way to locomotives. The first of these was delivered in 1833, just four years after Robert Stephenson's pioneering locomotive *Rocket* won the Rainhill Trials. At this time any railway, and especially that across the High Peak, was something of a novelty. It was also isolated from the rest of the rail network. Soon, however, a flurry of new lines was created and in 1853 one of them burrowed through Cromford and Buxton on its way north. This main line formed part of the Midland Railway's route from St Pancras station in London to Kettering, Leicester, Derby, and Manchester. Almost touching the High Peak line, it was probably inevitable that in 1853 a connection was made... at the splendidly-named High Peak Junction. Shortly afterwards in 1857, Whaley Bridge also found itself connected to the main railway network. Here the railway joined the Buxton to Manchester route – part of the London & North Western Railway, which eventually owned the High Peak line. Suddenly, with rail connections at each end, the High Peak railway was something more than a bridge between two canals.

At High Peak Junction, the Derby-Manchester line runs right to left, with a rather battered shed on the left. At this point there are two main lines, two loops and the Cromford & High Peak line. 30 April 1967.

The High Peak Line at Work

Although the canals provided plenty of traffic for the High Peak line, it also generated increasing revenue from the terrain through which it passed. This involved serving the many limestone quarries along the route, but the railway also became the lifeblood for other businesses and domestic residences in nearby villages; it became the centre point of its own micro-economy. One thing that this area of Derbyshire lacked was a decent water supply, and the Cromford & High Peak Railway provided that right through to its closure. Old locomotive tenders were filled with water from a source at Cromford and then towed along the route, providing sustenance for the steam locomotives and winding engines, but also for anyone else who needed water. When I last visited the line in early 1967, water tanks were still being worked uphill from Cromford and also filled at Buxton to supply the northern section of the line.

While the railway was admired for its tenacity and ingenuity, it was, to say the least, a very inconvenient and labour-intensive operation. At each incline wagons had to be manually attached to the winding rope with chains. They were disconnected from the rope at the summit and then coupled up to a locomotive until the foot of the next incline was reached, where the whole procedure was repeated. Descending the inclines also involved attaching the wagons to the cables.

It wasn't too long before improvements were made. The two inclines between Cromford and Sheep Pasture were made into one, and the winding house half way up was closed. As new locomotives became available, with more power, it became possible (taking a run to gain speed) to climb Hopton incline without the need for winding ropes. Further north, a deviation – one of several – was built to eliminate Hurdlow Incline. Then, in 1892, after the London & North Western acquired the line, a new link to the High Peak Railway was built from Hindlow to Buxton, and this was to have a dramatic effect on the future of the railway. By this time the role of connecting two canals had basically evaporated. The Buxton link meant that traffic generated by the line could now flow to the main railway system through either Cromford or Buxton. So the bold step was taken to abandon a large section of the northern route, from Ladmanlow to Shallcross and its inclines – surely one of the first big railway closures. The section from Hindlow to Ladmanlow was retained to serve a host of sidings on this part of the route. Ladmanlow itself also had a particularly busy yard.

The short section from Whaley Bridge to Shallcross, including the horse-worked Whaley Bridge incline, was retained to serve freight at Shallcross yard. With Hurdlow and Shallcross inclines abandoned, the railway went into the twentieth century with just three rope-worked inclines: Sheep Pasture, Middleton, and Whaley Bridge.

In the 1870s passenger services had commenced but, as you might imagine, they were somewhat tortuous for travellers (who were supposed to walk up the inclines) and the timetable was clearly a work of fiction. After a fatal accident this service was closed in 1877, but what a remarkable journey it must have been.

So the railway continued, providing revenue, firstly for the London Midland & Scottish Railway, who inherited it in 1923, and then British Railways, who took possession in 1948. The next closure came in 1952 when Whaley Bridge incline and the canal yard were shut down. As the wagons to and from the incline, like the incline itself, were worked by horses, this must have been a relief for BR, but it was the end of a great curiosity for the railway enthusiast. Shallcross yard had a separate link to Whaley Bridge station, so it was just the Peak Forest wharf that was shut down. Two years later the section from Harpur Hill to Ladmanlow closed. The Middleton incline carried its last wagons in 1963 and from that time the line was operated as two sections, with a declining amount of traffic: from Middleton Bottom to Cromford was one part and from Middleton Top to Friden and Buxton was the other.

The Railway in its Last Days

Even in its final years of operation, the line preserved its unique attributes. With just one incline in operation, from Cromford to Sheep Pasture, it remained a bucolic delight. The huge Middleton Quarry was still connected to the Cromford & High Peak Railway through the Sheep Pasture section of the railway. You could usually find a 'Kitson' 0-4-0 saddle tank working here, bustling around the quarry's timeworn corrugated iron buildings and conveyors, bringing hopper wagons of lime – usually carefully-sheeted – to Sheep Pasture ready for the descent to Cromford and then on to the main railway system via High Peak Junction.

The lengthy section from Middleton Top to Buxton seemed like a main line in comparison. Yet traffic was sparse, operated by the resident J94 tank engines from what was now the parent shed at Buxton (previously it had been Rowsley and then Derby). They handed over their trains at Friden to Ivatt Class 2 2-6-0s for onward transit. Crossings, even over main roads, were rudimentary; they usually consisted of a pair of creaky crossing gates, which were opened by the guard. An example was where it crossed the A5012 at Pikehall, currently considered one of Britain's more dangerous roads. It was worse when a J94 on the High Peak line popped out of the undergrowth pulling just a few wagons and a brake van with the guard holding up the traffic to allow it cross. Today's health and safety-minded managers would have had a fit, but I don't think there were any accidents. Where the old railway crossed smaller country roads, there were no gates at all; it was just a case of the driver stopping and getting waved across the road by the guard.

It was reported in 1966 that quarry traffic using the Sheep Pasture section of the line would switch to road vehicles early in 1967. By this time water tanks were still being moved, but generally the railway was short of business and closure was imminent. At last it succumbed, with the final trains – full of enthusiasts – touring the railway on 30 April 1967. Happily, the line's potential as a tourist trail was realised by some far-sighted individuals and it is now a great asset to the local economy, while giving visitors a chance to experience something rare in the history of the route – a chance to walk or cycle along this lovely artery through Derbyshire.

It came as something of a shock when Dr Beeching proposed closure of the Midland main line between Derby and Manchester, as it was then seen as a vital route. Today, despite the closure of the line north of Matlock, both Cromford and Whaley Bridge stations are still served by passenger trains.

Students of railway history should consult *The Cromford & High Peak Railway* by Alan Rimmer for the classic history of the line.

At Cromford the small shed on the left has gone but other buildings survive today, as does the water tower, seen here on a misty 13 April 1967 (Bryan Jeyes).

The Cromford & High Peak Railway's Historical Timeline

1825 – An Act of Parliament is granted to build a railway from Cromford to Whaley Bridge, linking the Cromford and Peak Forest canals.

1831 – The railway, including nine rope-worked inclines, is opened. Horses move wagons on the stretches between inclines.

1833 – Steam locomotives start to take over from horses on the level stretches.

1853 – The south end is linked to the new Derby to Manchester main line at High Peak Junction.

1857 – The north end is linked to the Buxton to Manchester railway at Whaley Bridge.

1887 – The London & North Western Railway, having leased the line, now acquires it.

1892 – A new line is built connecting Hindlow with Buxton and the section between Ladmanlow and Shallcross (near Whaley Bridge) is abandoned.

1899 – Parsley Hay becomes part of a new railway built from Ashbourne to Buxton.

1923 – It is absorbed by the London Midland & Scottish Railway.

1948 – It is now included in the new nationalised British Railways.

1952 – The short section from Whaley Bridge to Shallcross yard, including an incline still worked by horses turning a capstan, is closed.

1954 – It is the end of the line from Harpur Hill to Ladmanlow yard.

1963 – Middleton Incline is closed, severing the railway into two sections.

1967 – In April the railway is abandoned.

1971 – About seventeen miles re-opens as the High Peak Trail.

The Locomotives

Operating the Cromford & High Peak line was always a challenge. Historian Alan Rimmer says information on the line's early stock is rather meagre, but he does give quite detailed descriptions. You have to remember that these engines had to be hauled painstakingly up the gradients to their place of work in the early days (and, as far as Sheep Pasture is concerned, right to the end of the railway's operation). Rimmer identifies the first engine as an 0-4-0 named *Peak*, which probably ended up as a stationary engine at Cromford. It was followed by a 2-2-0 tender engine that was eventually rebuilt as a saddle tank that eventually finished its days shunting at Crewe. Once the line became part of the London & North Western Railway, standard types from that line were used – especially the 'Chopper' 2-4-0 tanks. They had a very long reign, one of them surviving on the line into BR days. Also employed were the LNWR 'Bissell' 0-4-2 tanks, so called because of their strange trailing truck. The 'Choppers' eventually gave way to the ex-North London Railway 0-6-0 tanks, which proved ideal. They had all the necessary ingredients for a good High Peak engine – lots of power, a short wheelbase, and easy maintenance. Plus, of course, a decent cab for those harsh winters (the very early types had no cab at all). When the North London engines were retired in 1960 they were replaced by modern J94 0-6-0 saddle tanks at Cromford and Middleton. Those in use during my time were 68006, 68012, 68013, 68034, 68068, and 68079. The J94s, built in the 1940s, shared with the North London engines ample power and a short wheelbase and they held sway at Middleton right to the end. By this time the Sheep Pasture section was worked by Kitson 0-4-0 saddle tanks, with Nos. 47000, 47006, and 47007 all seen in my days. The Kitson tanks were replaced with a 204 bhp diesel shunter in the last few months, one of which also took over from J94s shunting at Cromford.

Alongside the tank engines, Class 2 2-6-0 engines including No. 46401, 46465, 46480, and 46484 worked the lightweight freight trains between Friden and Buxton. The Class 2s were specially allocated to Buxton shed for this work, but also handled local trains from Chinley to Sheffield – some of the last passenger workings in the area hauled by steam. Their long-term High Peak predecessors had been the venerable Midland 3F 0-6-0s.

Diesel shunter No. D2377 was the last regular shunter at Cromford Bottom. Rumours that No. 47000, which was used on the Sheep Pasture section of the line, would be withdrawn in mid-1966 were unfounded but, at last, diesel shunter No. D2383 replaced the little Kitson saddle tank, which was withdrawn in October 1966. No. 47000 went to Derby and then on to Cashmore's at Great Bridge for scrapping – the end of many years' work on the line. It had first arrived at Sheep Pasture in 1952.

Another 'Kitson' tank, No. 47007, had been withdrawn at the end of 1963 – the first casualty among the class. It was cut up much closer to home, at Spondon near Derby. Sister engine No. 47006, also a Sheep Pasture regular, was scrapped at Cashmore's in October 1966 after withdrawal in August that year. Cashmore's received another High Peak regular, No. 68013, after withdrawal in August 1964. On 2 August 1966 a standard 350 hp 0-6-0 shunter, No. D3778, was given a trial over the northern section of the line with a 16-wagon load, but in the end the J94s soldiered on to the end. Maybe the diesel's brakes going down Hopton incline weren't up to the job.

On 31 March 1967 all rolling stock was cleared from Sheep Pasture and 0-6-0 diesel No. D2383 was lowered down the incline for the last time the following day. To mark the closure, an enthusiasts' brake van special ran on 4 March 1967 and another on 30 April when Nos. 68006 and 68012 were specially cleaned – quite a big job as they had been extremely grubby. Cashmore's scrapped No. 68006 when it was withdrawn in May 1967 following complete closure of the High Peak line. All that cleaning for the last day train, just for No. 68006 to be cut up! No. 68012 was in better condition and went to Westhouses shed for further service; I am not sure how much use they made of her, but she was certainly photographed shunting at Williamthorpe Colliery in North East Derbyshire in 1967. No. 68012 was taken out of service in October 1967 and sent all the way to Buttigiegs yard at Newport, South Wales, in January 1968 for breaking up. She was the last High Peak engine and the last of her class to remain in service.

Other Inclines

The use of inclines on Britain's railways was not exactly common, but there were more than one might expect. The Edge Hill Light Railway near Banbury had one graded at 1 in 6 (steeper than those on the High Peak line). It had no winding engine, but used weighted loads so the heavy downhill wagons hauled the empties uphill. Bryn Eglwys slate quarry at Abergynolwyn, at the end of the Talyllyn Railway, also had a steep incline. Rope-worked inclines were more common in the early days of steam engines, when the rather feeble locomotives were unable to climb gradients that later presented no problems. Until 1844, trains were hauled from Euston up Camden bank on a rope-worked incline, although it has been claimed this was because at the time regulations prevented steam locomotives from running closer to Euston, rather than their lack of power. Other rope-worked inclines included Dinorwic Quarry, Kit Hill, Calstock, Lee More, funicular railways, and even the Liverpool & Manchester Railway had a 1 in 48 incline to the docks at Liverpool. If you want to see a rope-worked incline in action today, the Bowes Railway in Durham still has one – the last standard gauge rope-worked incline in the world.

The Character of the Line

Even today, fifty years after the line closed, it is not hard to discover its unique character. We see a railway where a railway ought not to go – up hills and across ridges, while studiously avoiding villages and any other centres of population that might contrive to offer potential revenue from passengers. This was a line that, despite its ancient origins, had no pretensions to become the maid of all work that so many lines saw as their destiny. We can laugh today about lines that go from nowhere to nowhere and, indeed, my passion is for certain of these. We can celebrate, for example, the humble Northampton & Banbury Junction Railway, which had an ambitious title, yet reached neither Northampton nor Banbury. We can admire the fortitude that created the Midland & Great Northern Joint line, that strode ambitiously – albeit with a single track – from somewhere in the East Midlands to Great Yarmouth. But the Cromford & High Peak was much cleverer than that. It was entirely purposeful, seeking to link two canals as a kind of lengthy, rambling bridge might link two roads attempting to cross a river, and when the duty of linking canals became redundant it found enough freight along its route to keep it in action for 136 years.

If the Cromford & High Peak delighted in being one of the earliest of British railways, it also had to concede its rather ignominious status as one of the first to undertake a closure. However, the fact that it was still at work when many more important lines had thrown in the towel says much for its unique ability to serve geographically-challenged local businesses.

The Cromford & High Peak Railway Today

Let's take a ride on the Cromford & High Peak line. Not possible? Of course it is – you just need your legs rather than a locomotive and wagons. Or, take your car and stop at the conveniently placed car parks along the route. You'll still get a great sense of the railway's characteristics. Of course, when the line was running, we usually walked and if you are visiting the line today I hope you will find the comparison between what you see now and the pictures in this book fascinating.

Few railways that closed in the 1960s have survived better than the Cromford & High Peak line. The acquisition by Derbyshire County Council of more than half of it and open access to much of the rest has protected it in a way that means later generations can gather a powerful sense of what the railway was like. With a bit of human power and a bicycle, you can complete the journey from Cromford to Dowlow, near Buxton, a lot quicker than was ever possible by train. But if you want the best experience, I suggest you walk it; only then can you really take in some of the detail that makes the landscape and the industrial archaeology come alive.

We will start at Cromford Bottom. For some strange reason, this location has been renamed High Peak Junction, even though this is actually the title of the rail link with the Midland Main Line about a mile away. No matter – someone in the visitor centre is happy to give us historical information, sell us drinks and snacks, and cheerfully opens up the old workshops so we can peer at the fascinating artefacts here. These include a spare cylinder and parts of a flywheel from the Middleton Top beam engine. Also on view is a piece of ancient track cast with the letters 'C & HPR Co'. We had seen these back in the 1960s and thought they were extremely rare, but we found several more on display during our day.

For this exploration I am back with my friend Bryan Jeyes, with whom I made a number of trips to watch and photograph the line in its working days. It feels strange to return to a site we know so well and to see it looking in some ways the same, but radically altered in others. We notice that a section of the once-derelict canal has been restored and has a horse-drawn narrow boat carrying tourists. In the old days it was weedy and neglected, but in a rather leafy, attractive way. In other words, not full of road cones and supermarket trolleys. However, it seems that there has been some controversy about this canal restoration. Some feel it was caught up in the passion and momentum for canal rebuilding that swept through the country from the 1970s onwards; they feel it should be left to lie in isolated, derelict, and enchanting peace.

'Fully restored and completely unused', said writer Paul Atterbury after its restoration and he had a point. Much of the restoration hasn't lasted. A storm damaged the embankment and made the route south unnavigable, so currently nature has had the final say and the short section at Cromford is all that remains in use. A stroll around this canal still contrives to be a relaxing location for contemplative reflection.

One canal feature that Bryan and I are delighted to see restored is the dramatic Leawood Pumping Station, with its lovely old beam engine. Once you could see this elegant structure quite clearly from the surrounding area, but the onward march of trees and undergrowth has somewhat sheltered it from view. It pumped water from the River Derwent to the canal and still does on steaming days. Such is the remarkable setting for the start of the railway. Almost opposite the pump house are the old wharves, now turned over to residential purposes, but retaining their vintage charm. In the old days there were often wagons around here either waiting to be moved towards High Peak Junction (the real one!) or uphill to Sheep Pasture and beyond. Way back, goods were trans-shipped from boat to railway at this point.

'Everything here still has the same feel,' I observe. 'The canal, the lovely hills, the pump house, the visitors' centre – it's really very well done.' But I do notice that the engine shed, which was placed alongside the canal, has disappeared. It had a large side door so once offered access to load boats on the canal. Maybe it was built as something other than an engine shed.

We then inspect the bottom of the first incline that led to Sheep Pasture. Here we see an old pulley wheel around which the ropes turned as the descending rope quickly became the ascending rope. Some sections of rail and well-produced information boards show how the inclines were operated. There is a pair of LMS brake vans to give it that authentic feel. The old water tower survives, as does the signal post, which has sadly lost its arm. Also in situ is an indicator that once told the railwaymen when wagons were moving on the incline.

We examine the neat arch under the main A6 road, about twenty metres up the incline. It looks much too small for one train to pass beneath, let alone double tracks.

'It was rebuilt when the A6 was improved,' says our guide at the visitor centre. It's in keeping, however, with the surroundings. As we climb the incline, the first point of interest is the catch pit. Unchanged since the line was in use, this was a refuge into which runaway wagons could be diverted by the brakeman situated a little further up the incline. Inside was the same wrecked wooden plank wagon that was there in the 1960s, now looking much the worse for wear. The points were spring-loaded and set to the catch pit. The pointsman, therefore, had to divert wagons away from the pit once he was satisfied they were not runaways. Alan Rimmer reports that the last 'runaway' down the incline was in 1965 when two wagons were wrecked in the crash pit. One of them must be the wagon that is there to this day.

'My instinct would be to leap over the wall if a loose wagon came flying down the incline,' I say. 'Never mind standing here fiddling with points.' This is an unhelpful observation, as many years ago before the catch pit was built, a runaway wagon raced down the incline and flew across both the canal and the main railway line. It could have been a major disaster had it hit a train on the main line.

The incline to Sheep Pasture represents the toughest part of the High Peak trail for both trains and walkers. As it was originally two inclines – one at 1 in 8 and the other at 1 in 9 – it is long, but not too arduous, even for the gently unfit. Like me.

There is alas no 0-4-0 Kitson saddle tank waiting to greet you at Sheep Pasture, only the shell of the winding engine's house and some excellent views down to the valley below. Even that signal we spotted on our first visit has disappeared. A replica would be nice. The next interesting site is Black Rocks. Here the geology is the attraction. Black Rocks is above the High Peak Trail, with several walking routes to reach this spot, but the huge lumps of grit that stand alongside the track are also fascinating. The job of a driver on the Cromford & High Peak line was surely like no other, as they trundled wagonloads of quarry stone through spectacular countryside, once much more open than today's undergrowth-lined surroundings. A little further on is the National Stone Centre – did you know there was such a thing? We try a cup of tea here, where you can discover all about the geology of our world and even learn how to build a dry stone wall. Always handy.

Soon after this, we reach the base of the next incline, leading up to Middleton Top. Once there were sidings here, one of which went to Middle Peak Quarry. In fact, the railway served a number of quarries, with Middle Peak being one of the larger ones. It was once owned by Derbyshire Stone Group and before that Stewarts & Lloyds, eventually being taken over by Tarmac. For hundreds of years limestone was extracted from this area, later giving life to the High Peak railway. The siding to the quarry curved off to the left at the bottom of Middleton incline. As we ascend the incline, the nature of the trail changes; the lower half is enveloped in the inevitable undergrowth and the gradient is slightly less steep than that leading up from Cromford. Beyond here it is less enclosed and right in the middle is an impressive tall arched bridge, from which point there are open views. Comparisons between the scene today at Middleton Top and that in the 1960s shows what efforts must have been made then to keep the foliage under control, as you could see the engine house at Middleton from miles around. Now it is still a local landmark, but close up it is enveloped in the inevitable crop of trees.

This scene was very remote in working days, with few trees around. Today, Middleton Top has an excellent visitors' centre, but is much more overgrown.

Middleton Top Today

Middleton Top is one of the highlights of the route and was a busy place in the 1960s. Well, I say busy – actually there were simply wagons going down to the bottom of the incline and trains running north to Friden and on to Buxton, but there always seemed to be one engine in steam or on the move.

During late September, while High Peak Junction and Parsley Hay visitors' centres are open, Middleton is shut, but you can usually hire bicycles from here and grab some refreshments. I have to say it is odd wandering around, drinking in both tea and memories. The old Butterley winding engine that was used at Middleton right to the end is still there and is run (on compressed air) on certain days of the year. A wagon stands poignantly at the top of the incline and a signal has been erected, but with the arm facing the wrong way. Why would they do this? Yet, as we stroll around, it evokes powerful memories. Some Derbyshire County Council employees are working at the site and we get chatting.

'You have some old pictures? Wagons being attached... in colour? We'd love some of those for the county council archive,' says one of them. I take his email address, happy to oblige.

From Middleton Top it is a straightforward walk to Hopton Bottom, through a short but exciting tunnel. On Hopton incline the gradients seem comparatively gentle, but you have to remember that although it was initially operated as a rope worked incline, as more powerful engines came along it was found that they could reach the top untethered. Once an engine was derailed here due to the state of the track. The final two hundred metres are at a fierce 1 in 14 and that was the steepest climb worked by normal trains in Britain; until you've seen an engine thrashing up Hopton Incline, you haven't experienced the full atmosphere of steam railway working. Luckily there is some film available to recall the sights and sounds for those who missed out, whether by age or distraction, from seeing it for real. A road runs parallel with the incline. I recall it was crowded with cars on the railway's last day, back in April 1967, as we all raced the train. As with so many railways, alive and dead, undergrowth is taking over and blocking the once-open vistas. Limestone quarries here helped the railway's balance sheet and some is still extracted from this area – the last such quarry in Europe.

Bryan and I wander around the top of Hopton Incline, but as a former power station manager, his attention is drawn to the giant wind turbines that rumble and swish in the nearby fields.

'Maybe there is still a role for this old railway line in today's environmental age,' I suggest. 'After all, there are a number of quarries near the line and you could run tourist trains along the rails at weekends.'

Highly unimpressed, Bryan asks what you would do with the cyclists and walkers.

'Easy,' I reply. 'You just load them on to the trains. It would save them all the effort of walking and biking.' Bryan gives me a quizzical look and I start laughing.

At Longcliffe there were more exchange sidings and also the site of a rather crude, but fascinating water supply system. All steam locomotives need lots of water, and on the Cromford & High Peak line it was transported along the line in old tenders for locomotives, winding engines, and general domestic use. In fact, if you stood at the bottom of Cromford incline, it seemed that almost as many water tenders were going up the grade as mineral wagons. I gather the very last rail vehicles removed from the High Peak line after closure were antique water tenders. At Longcliffe a ramp was built so these old tenders could be pushed up to a higher level allowing gravity to feed water into the locomotives' tanks.

'Amazing that such a rudimentary way of filling water tanks lasted until 1967,' says Bryan. He's right, but a lot of old practices died hard on this unique railway.

From here, the High Peak Trail runs through very pleasant countryside to Minninglow, where it crosses a vast, dry stone wall embankment and then, after passing a free (!) car park, on to the very sharp Gotham Curve. This was the sharpest bend on any British main line railway and meant only short wheelbase engines and four wheel wagons could be used on the line. Time's getting on and we need to make progress. Our next stop (again with a car park) is Friden Goods where there is a huge brickworks that, until 1965, used the High Peak line for transport. After that it was lorries, but a mural and information boards tell the story of Friden Goods. We walk from here to Parsley Hay, about a forty-five minute stroll. The most interesting feature is probably the short Newhaven Tunnel with different inscriptions either side as you approach the junction at Parsley Hay. They are dated 1825, when King George IV was the monarch, George Stephenson was driving the first successful steam engine (*Locomotion*), and children were newly restricted to working 'only' twelve hours a day in cotton mills. This was the date of the Act of Parliament that permitted construction, the railway opening six years later.

A Junction for Ashbourne

Parsley Hay sees another former railway line approaching from our left – what is now the Tissington Trail. This was once the railway from Buxton to Ashbourne, which was an early (1963) casualty in the decline of Britain's railways. For many this is the start (or end) of their tour. The old signal box and station at Parsley Hay have gone; now there is a very friendly visitor centre where you can hire bikes, buy food and travel guides, and generally take a rest if you are walking or cycling. On this occasion we are not, of course, so after a pause we move on. There is another car park at Sparklow and if you stroll further on past Hurdlow you come to the point that is the end of the High Peak Trail, near the main A515. From here you can make your way to Buxton or try to follow the original route, some of which was closed more than a century ago. Parts of this are actually quite easy to see and it is possible to investigate much of the trackbed, although you'll need some deviations and to check rights of way. As time goes by, and more of the land has restricted access, it is likely to become trickier to follow the old route, but currently it's certainly not too difficult to at least get a good feel of this northern section. The one area of the Cromford & High Peak line still in use is here, linking Tunstead Quarry through Hindlow Tunnel to the railway network at Buxton.

The wild, moor-like nature has always seemed very different from the lush green dales scenery south of Parsley Hay. It has a splendour that makes it attractive and is certainly worth exploring, even if this means tracking the old line by road using a bicycle or car. At Hurdlow you can still see the old incline marked by a line of telegraph poles; it closed due to a deviation built as far back as 1869.

The railway ran north through Harpur Hill, where visitors can view a network of embankments of abandoned railway works. At Ladmanlow there isn't a great deal to see, but it is easy to locate the site of the old railway yard that was once so busy here. The route continues to Bunsall, which was where the railway started its descent, initially on two adjoining inclines. These have been converted into a road, but if you delve among the undergrowth at the bottom you can find the remains of a bridge and trace the route leading to the eastern edge of Fernilee Reservoir. This a wonderful place to be, with the reservoir actually never having seen rail traffic as it was built in the 1930s – well after the line was closed. Eventually the railway reaches Shallcross, where another incline drops the High Peak line down to what was once a busy yard and is now a small area of housing. You can easily trace the line in this area and there is a very helpful information board near the top of Shallcross incline.

Shallcross yard stayed open until 1966 using a spur to the Buxton to Manchester railway.

Bryan and I discuss a visit which was made to this cramped yard by no less than a Royal Scot Class 4-6-0 after its express days were over.

'You just cannot imagine squeezing such a huge engine into the yard here,' I observe.

'It must have been the biggest engine ever to touch the High Peak line, says Bryan, and that's true.

The original tracks ended at Whaley Bridge. Here they met the Peak Forest Canal, the original destination when the line formed a link between two canals. Whaley Bridge definitely has much to interest anyone wanting to find out about the Cromford & High Peak Railway. When we arrive there we find the old transit warehouses still in place and some old tracks half buried. The canal basin is still busy, used by tourists and pleasure boats. The incline itself can still be walked – it's short, but at 1 in 14 much too steep for adhesion-worked trains. It was here that, right until closure in 1952, wagons were hauled uphill by a horse-drawn capstan. Although most people today concentrate on the High Peak Trail, I would strongly recommend a visit to the northern end of the railway so you can get a feel of the spectacular countryside it crossed before the 1892 closure. The local authorities and other bodies have placed excellent information boards along the whole length of the line and they help to give visitors an idea of the remarkable engineering features of the railway.

A Line Like No Other

Whether you are a tourist seeking exercise among scenic delights or someone with an interest in industrial archaeology, the Cromford & High Peak Railway has much to offer. I hope that the following pictures – mostly taken in the last few years of its existence – give an idea of what a real curiosity it was. No great sense of completeness is claimed, but I have tried to source pictures from other photographers of one or two key places I missed, or photographed in black and white. The fact is that not too many colour pictures were taken in its working days. However, you can still see so much for yourself and this means that we have an inheritance that future generations can use and enjoy.

I am very grateful to those who helped me explore the railway both in its working days and now, and who helped with this narrative – Bryan and Pam Jeyes, Bob Mullins, Alistair Kohler, Nick Evans, and my wife Jane. Oh yes, and that tall lad on a train from Derby to Manchester...

To me, Ambergate station was always the gateway to the Peak District. It was a rare triangular station, set in rolling hills. This is the view from the south; the lines to the left ran to Cromford and Manchester and those to the right to Chesterfield. You can see the other platforms completing the triangle in front of the hills. I went back twenty years later after 'rationalisation' and it really was the most depressing sight. This view was taken on 30 June 1966.

Early morning at Ambergate on 3 August 1965 and Class 8F 2-8-0 No. 48336 is waiting in the mist for the road. Her freight from the Chesterfield line is standing on the north platform of this triangular station and, with a good head of steam, she is impatient to go. Taken from a train on the way to Cromford.

Running south near High Peak Junction, No. 92022 is an ex-Crosti 2-10-0 and once very familiar to me as it spent many years at Wellingborough. Here she is only four weeks from a heavy intermediate overhaul at Crewe, hence the smart paintwork. She is heading south near High Peak Junction, Derbyshire, on 3 August 1965.

33

This was our very last visit to the Cromford and High Peak Railway during its working days, which had occupied so much of our time in the previous four years. Aware that it was the last day, we wanted to take a few photographs that would never be possible again. High Peak Junction's Midland Railway signal box was a priority. Notice the immaculate bank, the neat row of fire buckets, and the signal with a sighting board. 30 April 1967.

High Peak Junction on 30 April 1967 with a southbound train due. The tracks on the right form the High Peak line. (Bryan Jeyes)

I am standing a few hundred yards from High Peak Junction where the Cromford and High Peak line is single track. On its way to Cromford Wharf it ran through beautiful scenery – less dramatic than the higher reaches, but very sylvan. The battered hut marks the point where the Derby-Manchester main line runs past with its mass of telegraph wires. 30 April 1967.

Between High Peak Junction and Cromford Goods, the line ran through woods which gave it an eerie silence, despite the close proximity of the Midland main line and the A6 trunk road.

35

This is the overgrown Cromford Canal and the transit sheds where at one time loads were switched from canal boat to the Cromford & High Peak Railway. A little Singer Chamois car is seen as well on 30 June 1966. The buildings survive today, with that on the right now used as residential accommodation. The Cromford Canal was still derelict at this time.

The warehouse buildings where narrow boats unloaded their merchandise for transport by rail across the Peak District to Whaley Bridge in the old days. They are seen here on 30 April 1967 with Leawood Pump House on the left across the other side of the Cromford Canal. We are looking towards High Peak Junction. The sign warns that engines must not enter the warehouse.

Latterly, a diesel shunter was used at Cromford. You can see the chimney of Leawood Pump House in the background. No. D2377 is assembling wagons for the climb to Sheep Pasture on 30 June 1966; notice the water-carrying tender behind, most likely an old LNWR locomotive tender.

Cromford locomotive shed was a sub-shed of Rowsley (17D) and later of Derby and Buxton, by then 16C. Inside the shed on 30 June 1966 is Class 0F 0-4-0ST No 47006, its duties being undertaken by sister engine No. 47000 on this day.

37

A general view at Cromford on the final day of the Cromford & High Peak Railway. The last wagons have come down the incline and a new life as a tourist area awaits. To the right, with the red door, is the engine shed. You can get an idea of the layout, with the first incline leading uphill to Sheep Pasture circling around the catch pit. Some wag has stuck a forty mph speed limit road sign on the very tall signal – four would be nearer the mark! 30 April 1967.

The fairly congested layout at Cromford Bottom can be seen here on 3 August 1965, with the centre track leading to the engine shed, containing 0-4-0ST No. 47006. The first incline ran uphill to the left of the building with the red door.

Today the main buildings still survive and you get a good feel of what it was like in working days. The coach body, engine shed, and tracks have all gone in this view taken on 27 September 2016, but the red gates survive with the workshop behind.

Leawood Pump House, Cromford – a rather esoteric view of the elegant chimney on 30 June 1966.

Canals needed water and the difficulty in providing it was a key reason for building a railway across the Derbyshire hills, rather than a canal. Leawood Pump House, which provided water for the Cromford Canal, has a stately elegance that adds to the Cromford Canal and railway scene on 30 June 1966. The building stands right beside the Cromford Canal.

This picture links the bottom of the first incline with the transit warehouses and Leawood Pump House and was taken on 30 April 1967. Despite the special 'last day' train at Middleton Top, nobody else was taking photos of the wharf and bottom incline, so we had the place to ourselves. On the right is an old LNWR tender converted to a water carrier.

This view is looking up from Cromford Bottom towards Sheep Pasture on 3 August 1965. This was the beginning of the Cromford & High Peak Railway, where we spent many happy hours. It steepens to 1 in 8 farther up the hill. The weedkiller train arrived soon after.

The workmen have now attached the first pair of wagons to the rope and they are about to commence the ascent to Sheep Pasture on 30 June 1966. I suspect this scene, apart from the weeds, had not changed much in many years. The buildings on the right used to contain an old length of rail marked C&HPR, which was always shown to interested visitors. The water tank on the left, fed by a local source, still survives.

41

On 30 June 1966, a bright summer's weekday, we see wagons being attached to the steel rope at Cromford by chains, prior to their ascending the first incline.

A general view of Cromford, with the various stone buildings on the right, the water tower, and the tracks making an amazing change in gradient. Notice the neat row of fire buckets under the shuttered window. It looks very quiet, but the ropes were moving and descending wagons are about to appear. 30 June 1966.

Now two wagons that have been chained to the rope are starting to climb the incline and pass under the A6 road bridge at Cromford on 30 June 1966.

A pair of loaded, limestone-streaked wagons form the balancing load and they have passed beneath the A6 road bridge. Luckily 30 June 1966 is a lovely summer's day and working the line is a pleasure. We had come here a few weeks earlier and the weather was so cold and misty I had to shoot pictures in black and white.

This is the bottom of the first incline up to Sheep Pasture on 13 April 1967. You can see the rails suddenly climbing upwards beyond the water tower. Almost all the buildings on the right are still there today. (Bryan Jeyes)

At Cromford on 13 April 1967 we see the point where the uphill ropes reappeared after having rotated around a pulley wheel. These ropes are made from wire and the wagons were attached to them. It all looked a bit Heath Robinson but it worked fine for many years and, happily, this little section has been preserved. (Bryan Jeyes).

One of the more extreme gradient posts in the country was situated at Cromford, showing a change in grade from a modest 1 in 200 to a seismic 1 in 9! Of course, the 1 in 9 section was rope worked as an incline. 13 April 1967.

A view looking down the first incline to Cromford Bottom on 13 April 1967. This was the beginning of the Cromford & High Peak Railway. You can appreciate the dire consequences of a runaway wagon.

This view was taken from the bridge that carries the main A6 road across the Cromford & High Peak Railway at Cromford Wharf. Below, you can see the sheds and water tower. The next two empty wagons to ascend are being attached to the ropes. It's a very damp December day, which dulls the setting, but this was not atypical. A cheery fire glows in the workmen's hut – a building that has since disappeared.

Two wagons are ascending and even from the A6 road bridge we can hear the whirring of the cables. We gaze uphill to await the balancing load coming down of two more wagons. This was 21 December 1966 – a gloomy winter's day.

Once the ascending wagons went out of sight, it was only a very short time before those coming downhill appeared. The aggregate is limestone from quarries near Wirksworth. Houses on the right had a spectacular view of CHPR operations. Beside the track is the black cabin occupied by the pointsman ready in case of runaways. The road is the main A6 from Derby northwards and a GPO van is doing a spot of overtaking. Such damp weather is typical for December in this part of Derbyshire. (Bryan Jeyes)

The catch pit was lined with old sleepers. It was built after two wagons broke away in 1888, sped down the incline, and completely cleared the Cromford Canal and the Midland main line at the bottom. The points were normally set heading for the pit, but were changed by the pointsman when wagons were seen to be safely descending. A bell system warned him of 'runaways.' The gradient here is 1 in 8 – notice the angled pulley wheels on the curve and the quiet A6 main road.

47

During my time on the Cromford & High Peak, this wrecked wagon in the back of the pit was an ominous reminder that accidents could still happen. The same wagon is still there today! 30 April 1967.

One of several indicators positioned on the inclines, with this one still in existence. It shows B for Stand-by, S for Stop, and G for Go.

This is about halfway up the Sheep Pasture incline on 13 April 1967. Near here two inclines were converted into one.

It is 13 April 1967 and we are walking up the Sheep Pasture Incline. You can see it makes a slight curve. I suppose this would be about two-thirds of the way up.

When the Cromford & High Peak line was built, there were two inclines to Sheep Pasture, which were later amalgamated to be worked as one – just under 1,300 yards in total. The ruling gradient is about 1 in 8. Here we have the view uphill on what was once the second incline (and later the upper section of the first) on 30 April 1967. A separate winding house was once situated here. The patch of daylight in the centre is the top of the incline.

This picture was taken looking up the Sheep Pasture incline, running uphill from Cromford. You can see the ropes and pulleys and the top of the incline in the distance. 4 April 1967.

From a few yards short of Sheep Pasture, you get a feel of the inclines on the Cromford & High Peak line. This was a Saturday (3 August 1965) so we could walk up the incline in safety, although the engines were in light steam. Notice the catch points in case of a runaway wagon. The track was always a bit weedy in my day (the last four years of operation), but seemingly in good condition otherwise. Here we are looking downhill.

The old winding house at Sheep Pasture is still there today, but in later years an electric motor replaced the steam engine. Walkers today can breathe a sigh of relief at this point! Notice that the uphill line is above that descending.

We are now at the top of the incline looking down towards Cromford. Notice the gradient post, pointing level towards Middleton and 1 in 8 down to Cromford! The summer weeds are growing strongly. There are also catch points with a lever on the left in case of a runaway. 30 June 1966.

We have now almost reached the top of the first incline on the Cromford & High Peak Railway. This is another view downhill, not often recorded, with the rock cutting on the right on 30 April 1967. You can see the monument to the Sherwood Foresters at the top of the hill in the background. The Crich tramway museum now runs below that.

51

I'm now looking from Sheep Pasture down the first incline. As you can see, it's just like going over a cliff (3 August 1965).

This is the top of the Cromford incline and the ascending wagons have already been marshalled and hauled away. Notice the signal, which could be seen from the Derby-Manchester main line down below. The building on the right is the old winding house. There is also a sizeable water tank and the remains of the engine shed. It looks very quiet, but it was a working day and there were people about. A few minutes later a train arrived from Wirksworth. 30 June 1966.

The signal and circular water tank at Sheep Pasture, looking towards Middleton.

We waited awhile, and along came No. 47000 pushing some loaded wagons for descent in pairs. This little engine, ordered in 1932, gave great service over more than thirty years and is seen here busy at Sheep Pasture on 30 June 1966. The shunter gets a ride in the cab, with his pole across the buffer beam; just an everyday scene, which would be gone twelve months later.

The little Kitson-built tank engines were long-term residents on the Cromford & High Peak Railway. Here, on 30 June 1966, No. 47000 is at Sheep Pasture marshalling wagons ready to descend to Cromford. Having brought them from the quarry, No. 47000 is propelling them to the top of the incline to descend in pairs with shunters standing by.

On 3 August 1965, Class 0F 0-4-0ST No. 47006 is busy at Sheep Pasture on a day when working the line was a pleasure for the crews.

The wagons have now descended and the little Kitson engine – by this time the smallest (standard gauge) engine left on BR, I think – is running backwards to the top of the incline on 30 June 1966. One shunter hangs on for a ride, while three other men get ready for action as wagons are coming uphill.

I always liked these little Kitson tanks. Although the same size as an industrial tank engine, they had an altogether chunkier, more business-like look – probably due to their black livery and lack of cleaning. This one is the version built in 1953 with larger side tanks and was a Cromford & High Peak regular in later years. This picture was taken on 3 August 1965 at Sheep Pasture. No. 47006 is in steam and well coaled-up.

55

A close-up of the Sheep Pasture engine, No. 47000. She had been on this line since the early 1950s. Her shed plate says 16C, which was Derby. Sheep Pasture was a sub-shed of Derby at this time, 30 June 1966. Behind the wall is a gentle slope down to Cromford village and the Derby-Manchester main line.

This was a familiar view to those who worked at Sheep Pasture. It gives some idea how high up the line was, compared with Cromford village and the Derby-Manchester main line some 500 feet below. 3 August 1965.

Having moved some ascending wagons out of the way, No. 47000, with a very good head of steam, is about to shunt the wagons on the right to the top of the Sheep Pasture incline on 30 June 1966.

56

This delightful old crane still existed back in the 1960s, lurking in the foliage at Sheep Pasture.

This is the track heading north from Sheep Pasture and a cloud of steam in the distance would provide the first sight of an approaching train. It is hard to imagine that this railway is hundreds of feet above sea level. (Bryan Jeyes)

As it was the last day of the Cromford & High Peak Railway, I tried to fill in my photographic gaps. One of them was the water tank at Black Rocks near Steeplehouse Goods, seen here with Bryan (looking very dapper with his brolly) giving the structure some scale. This view is typical of the scenery between Sheep Pasture and the bottom of the second incline. At this point the line is 750 feet above sea level. (30 April 1967.)

Water was always a precious commodity on the High Peak line and a lot of effort was made to transport it along the line. Here, at Black Rock in 1966, the piping probably diverts water from a stream to keep the tank topped up. (Bryan Jeyes)

This picture, taken on 30 June 1966, shows the section between Sheep Pasture and Wirksworth Goods near Black Rocks. The track looks pretty overgrown, but No. 47000 had no problem forging through the weeds. The rocks ahead look appropriately named! A few years earlier the track here looked very tidy.

We are now on our way to the bottom of the Middleton incline. In the distance is the Black Rock water tank and those are pretty fierce curves, although well within the capability of the Kitson 0-4-0ST No. 47000, the regular shunter here. 30 April 1967.

Just ahead is the foot of the Middleton incline, which was closed in 1963. The sidings serving the Middle Peak Quarry were in place right to the last day of the Cromford & High Peak Railway, and the track is in good condition. Buffer stops mark the point where wagons would have started to ascend the 1 in 8 incline and you can see Middleton Top winding house on the skyline, marking the top of the incline. Although there was plenty of activity at Middleton Top, we had this area to ourselves. 30 April 1967.

The track has recently been lifted on the incline up to Middleton Top, seen here on 3 August 1965. Compare this with the view if you walk the incline today.

A very hot 3 August 1965 sees us looking down the old incline. This incline closed in September 1963.

The top of the old Middleton incline in September 2016, complete with characteristic signal and wagon, is now a delightful part of the High Peak Trail.

On a bitter December day in 1966, J94 No. 68012 is taking on water prior to being stabled overnight. The rudimentary shutters on the cab protect the crew from the icy Peak District wind blowing that day. (Bryan Jeyes)

This pulley wheel still exists on the side of Middleton Top engine house where the wire rope enters the building – September 2016. Notice the brackets for fire buckets. (Pam Jeyes)

Here two J94s are prepared for the last Cromford & High Peak line train at Middleton Top. No. 68006 is taking on water and No. 68012 (behind) is ready to go and lead the train on 30 April 1967. The stately columns supporting the water tank were once part of a winding engine.

These two large boilers powered the winding engine at Middleton Top for many years and they are still there today. The engine was built in 1825 and worked right up to closure of the Middleton incline in 1963. 13 April 1967.

Seen on 30 June 1966, this old locomotive boiler supplied steam for the beam engine until the incline was abandoned in September 1963. It had taken over from the twin boilers mounted in the engine house.

Trains on the Middleton section of the Cromford & High Peak line always had a brake van – in fact, sometimes the train was a brake van! In latter days this LMS vehicle was used, seen here at Middleton Top on 13 April 1967, a few weeks before the line closed. Now two similar brake vans can be seen at the visitors' centre at High Peak Junction.

A general view of Middleton Top on 13 April 1967. The top of the incline is just behind the winding house. 0-6-0ST No. 68012 can be seen in its roofless shed.

At the summit of Middleton incline was another remarkable gradient post, showing 1 in 8 downhill. The northerly gradient of 1 in 1,056 is basically level. 30 June 1966.

The usual engine, a J94, was on its way back from Friden. Some of the roof blew off in a gale a few years earlier – the same gale that destroyed the shed at Sheep Pasture. Later the roof disappeared completely. 30 June 1966.

Having trundled back from Friden, No. 68012 is now safely in her shed at Middleton Top. Although she looks in very poor external condition, she cleaned up perfectly for the last day services the following year. (30 June 1966)

For many years the old North London Railway 0-6-0Ts, with their short wheelbase, held sway on the High Peak line. The last to leave was No. 58850, seen here at Rowsley shed on 30 June 1960. Happily it was saved for preservation at the Bluebell Railway. (Gerald T. Robinson)

Middleton Top was always a very serene spot, over 1,000 feet high in the Derbyshire hills. I used to love these visits to watch the engines pottering around. The cabin on the right is at the top of the incline, while the engine shed is on the left. This was the scene on 30 June 1966.

The Middleton Top beam engine is seen here when the building was opened for us on 21 December 1966 following an official request. It gave 120 years of service. This was situated at the top of the Middleton incline.

Inside the workshop at Cromford (now rather confusingly called High Peak Junction) are these spare items for the Middleton Top winding engine – a cylinder and flywheel parts. The staff here will be very happy to show them to you.

J94 No. 68012 stands in the now-roofless shed at Middleton Top on 13 April 1967, its work completed. Note the elegant windows to the shed. It was our penultimate visit to the Cromford & High Peak Railway – the next visit was to witness the last train.

Her work done for the day, No. 68012 is being readied for an overnight stay at Middleton Top and here we see the fire being thrown out. Notice the rudimentary cab door. These were affixed during winter to protect the crew against days like this one on 21 December 1966, when it was biting cold. It's the shortest day of the year and getting gloomy at three o'clock.

No. 68012 has been brought alongside the water tank at Middleton Top on 21 December 1966. The tank will be filled and then the crew will shut her down for the night.

69

Prestwich Intake Quarry, seen here in 1966, was once served by a siding from the High Peak line near Middleton Top. A thousand gallons of water a day were brought here by the railway in water tank wagons.

It must have been a massive effort to get 68012 this clean compared with the rust-covered machine I photographed a few weeks earlier. Sporting a York shed plate (it was actually allocated to Middleton Top, a sub shed of Buxton) she stands ready to lead the last day Cromford & High Peak special on 30 April 1967. Note the dented dome cover. The old Middleton Top shed with its strange Gothic windows has lost its roof, compared with my shots a few years earlier.

70

The south portal of Hopton Tunnel – one of three on the line – on 30 June 1966, with a J94 due shortly from Friden. These days you can enjoy walking or cycling through here.

This picture shows how the chimney of Middleton Top engine house was quite a landmark from around the area. Trucks from local quarries were a familiar site, hence this Dodge vehicle from Harry Evans (no relation!). This was on 13 April 1967 and this view is from the A5012. In the end, competition from lorries finished off the High Peak line.

The last day special train near the summit of Hopton Incline with the two tanks blasting past giving an impressive show to an admiring audience (Ted Baxendale, courtesy of Kerry Parker).

71

We are looking down Hopton Incline, the steepest adhesion-worked railway in the UK. As the gradient post says, the incline, once roped-worked, is at a horrendous 1 in 14. At the bottom, the line curved left towards Hopton Tunnel.

This is a view towards the top of Hopton Incline on 30 June 1966, with the line climbing at 1 in 14 before levelling out on its way to Friden and Parsley Hay. Cyclists today can relax in another few yards.

The two engines on the last day Cromford and High Peak special are about to pass me, but that was almost as far as they got. The pair of engines and six well-filled brake vans stalled on the 1 in 14 gradient a few yards farther on. Notice the unauthorised passengers in the cab on 30 April 1967. This picture was used as a front cover on *Railway World* magazine many years ago.

The two J94s have reversed cautiously down the grade and the six brake van train has been divided into two sets of three. The first of these now makes its way up Hopton Incline and this time the 1 in 14 grade is no problem. You can see the line swinging left towards Middleton Top and the three remaining brake vans at the bottom of the incline as 68012 and 68006 furiously begin their next assault. You didn't need to go to Shap for impressive steam action! 30 April 1967.

With the top of the 1 in 14 gradient in sight, the two J94s blast past on 30 April 1967, now with just three brake vans. Notice the apparel selected by fellow enthusiasts and the old bus which had brought a group of people to the site. We even have two women with cameras!

73

With only three brake vans in tow, the two J94s now have no problem climbing to the summit at Hopton.

For the third time, the two J94s are blasting up Hopton Incline, this time with the second portion of their six brake van train. I decided to move nearer the summit and watch them from the road.

74

The end of a magical, if sad day. The two J94s have now descended Hopton incline on their way back to Middleton and contribute to a wonderful vista of this area, with an old Austin Healey Sprite for company. (Ted Baxendale, courtesy of Kerry Parker).

Hopton Incline today still proves a challenge, but only for unfit people like me. It's hard to imagine steam engines shattering the peace and blasting uphill with a freight train. Time marches on and so does vegetation, which has changed the character of the line, but it was still lovely to go back here in September 2016, fifty years after those early exploits.

75

A section of old cast-iron fish-bellied track from the High Peak Railway and a sculpture made of oolitic limestone on a sandstone base now stand at Hopton. (Pam Jeyes)

Returning to Middleton Top with a brake van on 30 June 1966 is 0-6-0ST No. 68012, seen here near Longcliffe. This picture was a hasty one: we were driving along, saw the engine, stopped the car, and took a quick photo – hence the poor positioning of the engine.

Nos. 68006 and 68012 at Longcliffe. Despite the fact that they had taken water at Middleton Top, only about five miles away, they needed a refill after their strenuous efforts at Hopton. (George Woods)

76

Here's a neat way to provide a water supply. Two old locomotive tenders have been pushed up a ramp at Longcliffe and are used to form a kind of mobile water tank. The character of the scenery is much more open at this point. (George Woods)

I have struggled to find a 1960s colour picture of the embankment at Minninglow, so here I resort to a modern view. Luckily, the scene has not changed too much over the years. These are dry stone walls and if you are on the High Peak Trail it is worth stopping to examine this wonderful piece of early railway engineering. In operating days it was lined with telegraph poles.

This is the line heading north between Minninglow and Gotham Curve on a perfect autumn day. Now the High Peak Trail, the railway is better known today than it ever was when working.

At 2.5 chains, Gotham Curve was one of the sharpest on BR at the time. It was the reason why only four wheel wagons were allowed on the Cromford & High Peak line and you can see a check rail. A J94 going round here really got the wheels screeching.

This is not meant to be a 'then and now' book, but I hope you will agree that this is an interesting contrast. Quite honestly, at Gotham not much has changed. The Cromford & High Peak Railway swung through about ninety degrees on its way from Longcliffe to Minninglow. Today walkers and cyclists use it every day as part of the High Peak Trail without ever thinking 'Did a railway really run around a bend this tight?' Much of the High Peak line was – and still is – lined by stone walls. 25 October 2016.

A wintry picture of No. 68006 with cab side sheets to keep out the cold and hauling two tenders and a brake van, possibly at Friden. (Ted Baxendale courtesy of Kerry Parker)

Emblems on either side of Newhaven tunnel recall the history of the line. This one commemorates Josias Jessop, who was the engineer in charge of building the railway.

Even today a few legacies of a working railway can be found, such as this old signal post just south of Parsley Hay.

The delightfully named junction at Parsley Hay on the High Peak line was where the Ashbourne line turned right. The left signal gave access to the line to Middleton Top, seen on 13 April 1967. A train is signalled from the Ashbourne line. You can appreciate what a remote spot this was in the old days.

Parsley Hay signal box – there was also a station here. Swinging off to the right on an embankment is the line to Ashbourne, while the Cromford & High Peak line turns left through Newhaven Tunnel. This was a pretty gentle, but lonely outpost for any signalman. Notice the heap of coal and the vital water churn. Water was brought to various points along the line by train. This point is now the 'junction' of the Tissington and High Peak Trails. 30 June 1966.

These are the old platforms at Hurdlow station on 13 April 1967. The station closed in 1949 and today this is basically the northern end of the High Peak Trail, but the platforms have gone.

81

Right next to Hurdlow station is the Royal Oak pub. I took this picture back on 13 April 1967. It was a day when we were taking photos of the Cromford & High Peak line and I assume we stopped here for light refreshments. Outside the pub is a 1964 Morris Oxford, a 1965 Ford Anglia, and a sign saying 'please park prettily.' Offilers Ales is a Derby brewery that closed in 1966. Through the trees on the right can be glimpsed Hurdlow incline.

Most stations have a pub nearby and this is Hurdlow in 1966. Then, as now, the Royal Oak is handily placed, but the platforms disappeared long ago. (Bryan Jeyes)

Despite being closed in 1869 when a deviation was built to avoid it, Hurdlow incline, marked by a line of telegraph poles, is still very easy to identify. It can be found behind the Royal Oak pub. 24 October 2016.

Harpur Hill featured a network of sidings that were in use serving quarries and other industrial sites. It was also the scene of a long deviation. You can see how much wilder the landscape is here.

At Ladmanlow there was a busy freight yard. Once the Cromford & High Peak Railway abandoned most of the northern section in 1892, this became the farthest point of operations from Cromford. It was kept busy into the 1950s. There were several sidings serving local businesses. This is the view today.

Burbage Tunnel is on the section that was closed in 1892 from Ladmanlow to Shallcross. Yet, in 1966, when I took this picture, most of the old route north of Ladmanlow was very easy to trace. The tunnel was 592 yards long – the longest on the line – and even back in 1966 it had been bricked up.

Despite being closed in 1892, the old line here near Bunsall Top is very visible and enjoyed by walkers. The wild, moor-like scenery contrasts with the leafy areas further south.

Taken on 13 April 1967, this picture shows the route of the High Peak Railway on the section near Bunsall Top that was abandoned as long ago as 25 June 1892. Even after seventy years the route is very clear. My little Fiat 600 is in the foreground, near where the current Goyt Valley car park is located. (Bryan Jeyes)

This old view shows the superb countryside traversed by the Cromford & High Peak line. Bunsall, seen here, was part of the section abandoned in 1892, but still clearly visible on a misty 13 April 1967. It had two inclines, which are now a road, here newly completed. In the distance is Fernilee Reservoir, with the track of the railway running along the right hand shore as viewed from here.

85

We are looking down the one-time incline to Fernilee Reservoir. The Cromford & High Peak line ran down what were two connecting inclines then headed alongside the reservoir (although in the railway's working days, the reservoir was not there, as it was built in the 1930s). Compared to the earlier view, the whole hillside has become covered with foliage. These railways were closed in 1892. (24 October 2016).

THIS ROAD WAS BUILT IN 1967 ON THE
BUNSALL INCLINE OF THE
CROMFORD AND HIGH PEAK RAILWAY
CONSTRUCTED 1831 ABANDONED 1892
MAXIMUM GRADIENT 1 IN 7
PRESENTED BY MEMBERS OF THE
STEPHENSON LOCOMOTIVE SOCIETY
1972

No need for comment – this sign is at the bottom of the road that was Bunsall Incline. It's a nice touch.

The High Peak Railway runs along the eastern edge of the reservoir. In its operating days, there was no water here and this was fields; the line ran along a shelf on its way from Bunsall Bottom to Shallcross Incline. It's all still easy to see, 120 years after closure. (24 October 2016).

Shallcross Incline descended to Shallcross yard on the section of the Cromford & High Peak Railway closed in 1892. It was situated just south of Whaley Bridge and was 817 yards long, graded at 1 in 10.25. This is the top of the incline on 13 April 1967.

87

Shallcross incline was slightly less steep than the others. It is on the section of the CHPR abandoned on 25 June 1982, but the sidings at the bottom were still in use in the 1960s, near Whaley Bridge. On 13 April 1967, I am standing on the incline. (Bryan Jeyes)

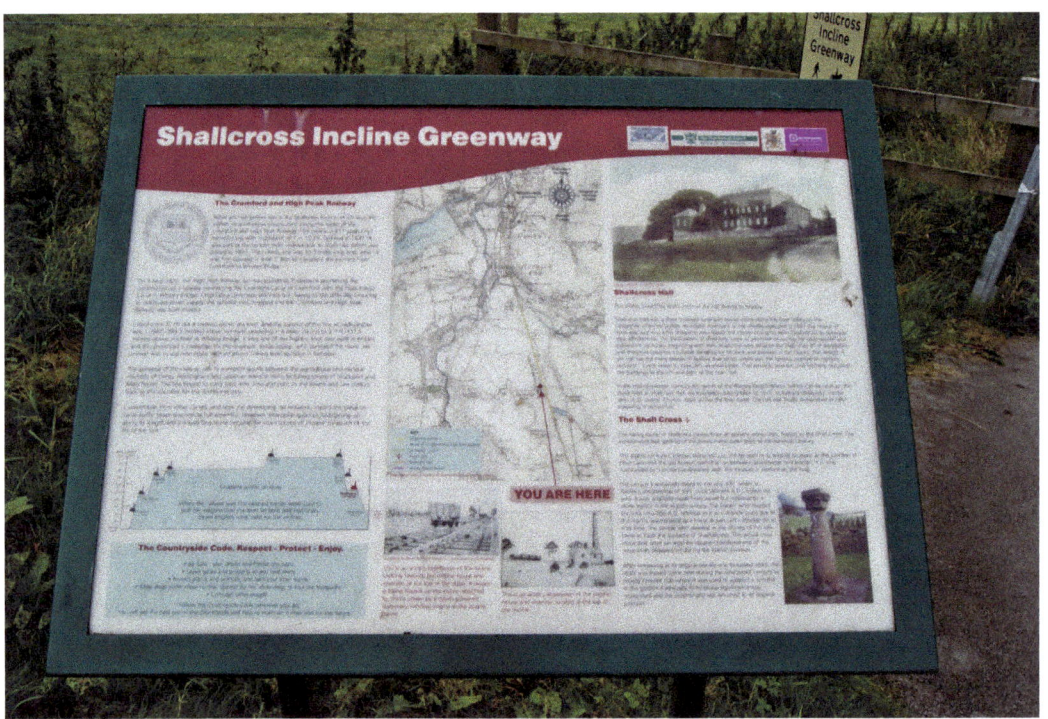

Even inclines that disappeared more than a hundred years ago now have explanatory signs, giving a good insight into the history and purpose of the old railway. This one is at Shallcross.

We are at the bottom of Shallcross incline on 24 October 2016, at the start of the section abandoned in 1892.

Another section that was abandoned before final closure, but this time on 9 April 1952 was Whaley Bridge incline. It started in the town and ran uphill at 1 in 13 and was very short. Today the church is concealed by trees. It is seen here on 13 April 1967.

At Whaley Bridge the gradient was 1 in 13 and it was less than 200 yards long. Horses pulled capstans to haul wagons up and down. This view was taken on 13 April 1967 with the transit sheds just visible (top right). Today you can still walk it and read excellent information boards.

The incline at Whaley Bridge has a cover of trees and has rather lost its railway feel. Here we are looking down towards the transit sheds on 28 September 2016.

This fascinating sign was situated near the bottom of Whaley Bridge incline. It reads 'CAUTION – KEEP CLEAR OF THE RAILWAY WHEN THE BELL IS RINGING AS WAGONS ARE MOVING ON THE INCLINE.' I took this picture on 13 April 1967 – the sign had survived for fifteen years since this section closed.

Here we have the River Goyt and the railway crossing it on a delicate bridge that still exists in Whaley Bridge – almost the north end of the Cromford & High Peak Railway on 13 April 1967.

This is the same old bowstring bridge, with rails still in place on 24 September 2016. In operating days this section was horse worked. Any visit to the Cromford & High Peak Railway today is incomplete without seeing Whaley Bridge.

91

Journey's end – these are the transit sheds for offloading between railway and canal at the north end of the Cromford & High Peak Railway, where it joined the Peak Forest Canal. You can see the central arch into which the canal flowed here on 13 April 1967. (Bryan Jeyes)

The Cromford & High Peak Railway transit sheds today, still in excellent condition and showing a date of 1832; In fact they look rather better than they did in the 1960s. Rails ran into each of the outer sections of the building, with the canal in the centre.

The other side of the transit sheds is seen here with the basin of the Peak Forest Canal. It has been landscaped and is a delightful area for a stroll. Notice the working canal boat moored on the right. And so our journey ends... almost! (Pam Jeyes)

A BRCW diesel multiple unit is standing in Whaley Bridge station on 17 June 1983. This was an LNWR line, hence the design of the signal box, although plunged deep in Midland Railway territory. These Class 104 units were the regular motive power at the time between Manchester and Buxton. From here there was a line leading to Whaley Bridge yard.

Looking very clean and freshly coaled inside Buxton shed on 30 June 1966 is this neat little Ivatt Class 2 2-6-0 No. 46465. She was the first of a batch built in 1951 at Darlington and was based at Buxton to handle local passenger trains and freights to Friden on the Cromford & High Peak line.

93

Simmering at Buxton shed (9D) on 30 June 1966 is Class 9F 2-10-0 No. 92023 — a former Crosti boiler engine. Buxton always had a good allocation of steam freight engines to handle traffic from the quarries and limestone plants in the area. This engine was a visitor from Birkenhead.

Trains still run on a short section of the old Hindlow-Buxton line for limestone processing. In the bucolic surroundings of the High Peak, No. 66183 accelerates away from a speed restriction towards the distant village of Harpur Hill with the early running 13.15 Briggs Sidings (Dowlow) – Ashbury's aggregate train on 4 August 2014. (David Hayes)

In this dramatic view, DBS Class 66 No. 66055 glints in the sun as it hauls 1,600 tonnes up the grade at Harpur Hill with the 11.08 Tunstead – Briggs Dowlow loaded limestone train on 29 December 2015. (David Hayes)

On 12 September 2016, Freightliner No. 66614 slowly lifts the 11.08 Tunstead to Briggs limestone train through the outskirts of Buxton along the green tracks around these parts. To the right of the loco is the remains of an old telegraph pole, which, unlike most of them on this line, never got removed. (David Hayes)

Bibliography

Atterbury, P. *Exploring Britain's Canals* (London, Harper Collins, 1995)

Hudson, B. *Through Limestone Hills* (Yeovil, Haynes Publishing Company, 1989)

Jones, N. and Bentley, J.M. *Railways of the High Peak Vols. 1 and 2* (Book Law/Foxline, 1997/2000).

Longworth, H. *British Railways Steam Locomotives 1948 – 1968* (Hersham, Oxford Publishing Company, 2013)

Marshall, J. *The Cromford & High Peak Railway* (Leeds, Martin Barstow, 2011)

Nicholson, C. P. *Branch Lines in the Peak District* (Clapham, Dalesman, 1977)

Potter, H. *The Cromford Canal* (Stroud, The History Press, 2009)

Rimmer, A. *The Cromford & High Peak Railway* (Lingfield, The Oakwood Press, 1962)

Rimmer, A. *The Cromford & High Peak Railway* (Usk, The Oakwood Press, 1998)

The Bowes Railway (2016) – http://bowesrailway.uk/rope/ Accessed 14 October 2016

Cromford and High Peak Railway *circa* 1958 (2016) – https://www.youtube.com/watch?v=A44_PjeBH2Y Accessed 14 October 2016

Sustrans – The High Peak Trail (2016) – http://www.sustrans.org.uk/ncn/map/route/high-peak-trail Accessed 6 October 2016

High Peak and Tissington Trails, Peak District National Park Authority (2016) – http://www.peakdistrict.gov.uk/__data/assets/pdf_file/0009/90486/hptisstrails.pdf Accessed 12 September 2016

High Peak Trail – Derbyshire County Council (2016) – https://www.derbyshire.gov.uk/leisure/countryside/access/walking/walks_and_trails/high_peak_trail/default.asp Accessed 4 September 2016

High Peak Railway Walks – the Goyt Valley. (2014) – http://theatreorgans.com/hammond/keng/kenhtml/High%20Peak%20Railway%20Walks/Whaley%20Bridge%20To%20Shallcross%20Incline.htm Accessed 20 September 2016

The Cromford and High Peak Railway by Tim Harris – https://www.flickr.com/photos/127577377@N06/albums/72157647342441905 Accessed 23 October 2016